JAMES MONTGOMERY FLAGG

I WANT YOU
FOR U.S. ARMY
NEAREST RECRUITING STATION

7th WAR LOAN **NOW··ALL TOGETHER**

OFFICIAL U. S. TREASURY POSTER

IF YOU WANT

To

FIGHT!

Howard Chandler Christy. 1915.

JOIN THE MARINES

GIVE IT YOUR BEST!

OFFICE OF WAR INFORMATION
POSTER NO. 9 · WASHINGTON, D. C.